A Mandala of Hands

A Mandala of Hands

Poems

John Warner Smith

Aldrich Press

ISBN 13: 978-0692415313

Cover art: "Circle Growth" by
          Dennis Paul Williams

          Photography by Philip Gould

Kelsay Books
Aldrich Press
www.kelsaybooks.com

Acknowledgments

Grateful acknowledgment is made to the editors and readers of the following journals where poems in this collection have appeared or are forthcoming:

About Place Journal: "Gazing," "Harlem the Morning After"
African American Review: "Rosa's Winter," "Sisters Mourning"
American Athenaeum: "Hunting Dragonflies"
Antioch Review: "Baptism"
Apalachee Review: "Krypton"
Bloodroot Literary Magazine: "Rain Dance"
Callaloo: "Crossing," "Letter to the Oaks"
Ellipsis: "Foghorn"
Fourteen Hills: "Memphis Soul Hour"
Kestrel: "An Artist Reflects on His Creations,"
    "Cries Beyond the Mountains"
Mom Egg Review: "Songs We Never Heard"
Pembroke: "Hand Fan"
Ploughshares: "Zydeco on Dog Hill"
Pluck!: "Samuel and Solomon, Age Six"
Quiddity: "Karaoke"
River Styx: "The Shaving Mirror"
The Worcester Review: "Talking Book"

I am indebted to the individual and collective gifts of all the faculty and poets of the *Callaloo* and Cave Canem communities. A very special "thank you" to poets Tracy K. Smith and Terrance Hayes for giving so generously of their time and talent, and to John Gery, Research Professor of English at the University of New Orleans, for his guidance and encouragement.

For my beloved parents and grandparents

Contents

Acknowledgments

Talking Book   11

ONE

Letter to the Oaks   15
Kiting   17
Plessy v. Plessy   18
The Prophecy of Sam Woodard   20
    (Louisiana, 1927)
How Did They Lynch Him?   22
Harlem the Morning After   23
Krypton   24
Atchafalaya   25

TWO

Rosa's Winter   29
Songs We Never Heard   30
Sisters Mourning   31
Ballerina   32
Three Creole Women   33
Mary Louella's Kitchen   35
Women of Rose Hill   36
A Cappella   37
Vigil   38

THREE

Hunting Dragonflies   41
An Artist Reflects on His Creations   42
Hand-Sewn Dolls   44
Cries Beyond the Mountains   45

Sands of Somalia   46
Samuel and Solomon, Age Six   47
Quicksand   49
The Girl Inside   50
Tree Poem   54
Picture Day at Mount Pilgrim, 1957   56

FOUR

Torched   59
Hand Fan   60
Gazing   62
The Shaving Mirror   63
Theinessen Pond   64
Tears   65
My Father's Treasures   67
Crossing   68
A Stranger Loss   70

FIVE

Rain Dance   73
Zydeco on Dog Hill   74
Memphis Soul Hour   75
My Brother's Flowers   76
Karaoke   77
Baptism   78
Foghorn   79
White Night at the Willow Lounge   80

SIX

Lessons Learned from a Teenage Daughter   83
Dream Walk   84
Blue Moments   85
Between After and Before   86
    (The House of Ernest and Mathilda)

About the Author

Talking Book

The pages of my book can part
like the sea. Their words move
my frost-bitten hands
like heat from a burning log
splintering to the pace
of my panting breaths.
Don't tell me to forget
the past you bury
with my dead, and embrace
this chattel hell, the price
you put on a looking-glass.
Why must I feed your fat heart
and sundown shadow creeping
a labyrinth of cotton blossoms
caging my humanity?
On this starless listening night,
I hear chants and drums
beneath my scorched earth.
I see ember kindling ashes
deep as the well of blood
you make and forsake. Here,
inside my hardened palms—
this is my past,
these are my dead.
Tonight, I'll tell *my* stories,
let them lift
the white-capped waves
like wind-blown snow
threshing your fertile fields.
Let water top your hills,
and the cage you build
be your own. Let my book talk.

ONE

I've known rivers:
Ancient, dusky rivers.

My soul has grown deep like the rivers.
—Langston Hughes

Letter to the Oaks

I. Charleston, 1863

Long before frost kissed
the shoal, before geese foretold
a miracle of raindrops congealing
on a mud pond,
you were the envy of maple.
In autumn you were ginkgo
beneath azure crisp and glazing.
Your fan petals fell
ripe in winter
with arms spread like sails
of the last slave ship
pushing off the coast of Gambia.
What bled and drowned
in the light of those
parched moons,
when they packed humans
in the bowel stench of a hold,
can never be redeemed,
never in your sweet shade
or under your crown of innocence,
when placenta dries
in a cotton field
and horse hoofs clop
on a hangman's road.

II. Birmingham, 1963

You were just a seedling,
tall and slender in girth
when you gave sanctuary
to newborn sparrows
who flew the geese flight.
The breath wind of slaves
seared your mama's boughs,
sent cries soaring moonward

over black waves
along the coast of Senegal.
And then the cataclysm.
Cannons ripped your green
swaying locks and rained
leaves, blood-soaked,
across two fields staking
their claim to your roots.
If there is time for truth
it is now, when you grow
old hearing beacon shrills
at dawn waking
birth of big dreams,
and you stand
the shifts of seas, mountains,
and human conscience.

Kiting

Tugging me, you ran
across the rain-drenched field
with boo weevils flitting
at your bare, white feet. Then,
lifting my thin wooden spine
and papier-mâché,
you fed me to the crosswind.
My trailing torn cloths,
knotted like ribbons tied
to a ponytail, snapped
like a bullwhip.
Rising, I felt the weight
of bone and flesh below,
anchoring me.
I felt your euphoria
of blood rushing
suddenly to your palm
as you parted the sunrays
with only a twig
and a ball of twine
held tightly in your hand.
As I spun and dipped,
the twine stretched,
bending like a bow string.
I prayed to tear away
when I started to climb
toward seven colors seen
arching the clouds
and touching down
in a dry, distant land.
But your taut line tightened.

Plessy v. Plessy

As white as Plessy was
in a shoemaker's apron,
he wasn't white
enough—
white enough, maybe,
by ebony keys he danced to
at Congregation Hall
or by tan hide soles he stitched
to London boots,
but still not white enough.

Plessy could never be
white enough
to ride first class in a railcar
or sit in the balcony
at Le Petit Theatre
and flaunt his ruffled
cuffs and cashmere frock.
On this Southern Comfort,
Jim Crow night,
not one colored child
would be lost in the stars,
not one
ounce of colored blood
would drip and not be heard
against the rails, rumbling
and clanging as they rolled.

Plessy could never be
white, not even in the mirror
of an octoroon ball
with its debutante sea
of Parisian silk gowns
and femmes de couleur

perfumed with the sweetest
water of New Orleans. Plessy,
for all his pallor
and panache, could never,
ever be white enough.

The Prophecy of Sam Woodard
(Louisiana, 1927)

I couldn't bear the sun's brightness,
so I stared blankly into the eyes
down below. The hangman tightened
the noose and tested the scaffold.
Then he draped a black sack
over my head. The trap door sprung
and I left Earth, suspended
between hell and eternity.
My neck bone snapped
and my eyeballs popped out.
Gasping for air, I kicked
and wheezed until I stiffened,
then I dangled like a thread.

With the noose around my neck,
they took me down. My heart
still pumped, so they pulled the rope
like a pulley and raised me up,
this time higher
above the gallows' floor.
They dropped me again.
They hung me twice, once
for killing a white man
in self-defense,
and again for dying too slowly.

But before the first drop, I heard
thunder blasting like canons.
I saw God spit
black clouds onto the ground.
Bones of every kind
floated down the Mississippi,
and moccasins nested
on the tops of tall pines.

I saw a rainbow
turned upside down,
and I told them: *If you hang me,*
you gonna see something
you never saw before.
But they hung me anyway.
They hung me twice.

How Did They Lynch Him?

Two cents for a piece of bubble gum.
That's what he went to buy.
Bye, baby. That's what they said
he spoke to the storekeeper's wife.

Like Herod's soldiers, they went,
darkness cloaked in moon glow,
and wrenched him from the stars,
stripped his mangled body
and dumped him in a river
to swell in sweltering Delta heat
and languish like old driftwood
in an unmarked grave
of bitter black mud.

Could have been a wolf whistle
he stuttered that cocked the rage
that felled the blows
that crushed his bones,
ground his meaty cheeks
into raw mottled mush
and gouged his hazel eyes,
dark as the pinewood box
they packed, nailed and boarded
for his last train ride home to mama.

Was it the bullet in his skull
or the gin fan hanging
from the barbed wire around his neck?
How *did* they lynch him?

Harlem the Morning After

By nightfall Harlem knew
who shot and killed the prince.
Mayhem and Molotov exploded.
Billy clubs and guns whipped rioters.
Someone bombed a mosque
and blew its roof off.

The next morning, like dripstone
in a cave, icicles hung
from verandas and zigzag stairs.
Amber glowed in street lights
as frozen as the siren and bell
of a parked red pumper.

Inside that crystal crevasse,
on the precipice of a winter storm,
a steel door slammed shut.
Silenced, Malcolm's words
soared from the bell towers
like a Sunday contralto.

Krypton

Jesse, everyone knew your shoes
never touched the ground,
but even you hadn't seen
a sprinter like Julio McGraw.

None bigger. A four-legged gelding,
so tall and fast they spotted you
forty yards. When the gun fired,
his start shook the ground.

His hoofs at your heels pounded
a locomotive in your ears,
but you crossed the finish first.
The race of the century,

you, an American in Cuba,
like Julio, without a country,
without honor. Black superhero,
I suppose we preferred myth

more than man, Krypton more
than Alabama. It must have hurt
to be a side show only months after
Berlin, your gold tarnished

like silver, unredeemable. Fame
didn't make you rich. Color kept you
poor, but your wings never broke
stride. You are ours for the ages.

Atchafalaya

Here, poor black men fish
or shove ice for the shrimp boats.
Women bear children, then work
where they're not seen, cleaning houses
and cooking in cafes across town,
bringing the ironing home
with a bundle of hand-me-downs
and leftovers for their own babies.

On workday evenings, they gather
in the quadrangle of small yards made
by the buckling, cross-shaped sidewalk
that connects their red brick duplexes,
government-built in the Eisenhower years.
In the air, the scent of beans, biscuits,
and pork fat, Motown and Memphis
blues blaring through the sheetrock walls.

Girls skip hop-scotch and rope
and spread handfuls of stars
to gather them before the rubber ball
bounces twice. Boys throw stick pegs
and crouch down in dust and twigs,
lagging and flicking glass taws.

Old soles, worn, heavy with troubles,
thin with hope, press against
the hand-drawn lines of Jim Crow.

TWO

Janie saw her life like a great tree in leaf
with the things suffered, things enjoyed, things done
and undone. Dawn and doom was in the branches.
—Zora Neale Hurston

Rosa's Winter

I.

Montgomery is blind
to the rock fault
that slips deep below
her jailhouse drone.
With strong winds whirling
overhead, she slow dances
in her daring,
careening in a waltz
through lazy mint julep days.
Her buses make black clouds
as they roll
down her fissured roads,
drowning the jingles
of caroling bells
and dimes trickling
fare machines.

II.

In no-man's-land,
Rosa sews a quilt
to warm her winter nights.
She cuts the buckling patches,
spreads them
across her hardwood floor,
then threads a pattern
of a young preacher
fanning hot coals, stirring
flames high as torch-lit crosses.
His cadence sounds
the beat of weary blues—
first a hush, a hum,
then foot-stomping thunder,
a swirling twister
of colored discontent.

Songs We Never Heard

Why, in her dying days,
did my grandmother thank us
for listening? We hadn't heard
the dew-drip taps of tears
that dropped to her pillow,

the thunder rumbling in her womb,
nor the curious soliloquy of cuss
and prayer that seethed through
her midnight-gritting teeth
as she paced the dusty hallways

dragging her feet with the burden
of hungry babies at her breasts
and Jim Crow on her shoulders.
We hadn't heard the soft rattle
of beads streaming through

her coarse hands that ached
as she prayed and bled
as she pushed a plow
or spun the sewing wheel.
When the trumpet blew, we

gathered freshly-cut flowers,
spread like a mort cloth of silk,
scented of frankincense and myrrh,
and walked her path, worn
with the weariness of living.

Recounting her days, we hummed
her Sunday songs in the fading
glow of her last sunset.
But we never heard the blues
our old black mothers knew.

Sisters Mourning

That year, the old sisters wore black in every season,
emptying hope chests like a roof-tearing twister—
so much to keep, so little to pass on. They must have sensed
fear flashing in their uteruses, and wondered

what locust larvae lay dormant beneath the goldenrod,
boring their tender limbs, reminding them
of limpid skies, how bound they were to things living.
Some days they gathered to celebrate the family—

Sundays in the sun, young lovers with nests
full of babies, old lovers with memories cradled
in their brows. Circled beneath a canopy of oaks,
they boiled blue crabs and crawfish in an open flame.

They told their stories with songs and black-and-white
photographs, between shuffled cards and dots counted
on small ivory stones. Now, four hand fans later,
the sisters speak of fallen branches. They take refuge

in beveled mirrors, in quiet times with questions
dangling in a slipknot. From their necks hang
hand-knitted scarves and the albatrosses
of pain not forgiven, salutations written but not sent.

Still, they wait to see patterns quilted for the spring
bazaar, the evergreens blooming in their winters.
Through the lives of their great grandchildren unborn,
they wait, silent about their steep climbs and falls.

Ballerina

for Antoinette Ruffin

The last time we talked,
you wanted to feel the crocheting rays,
so I wheeled you outdoors,
a short distance from the cinder block walls
you were given to live your last days.
It seemed a pity you had to lift
your un-blooming burden out of bed
and carry it with the lush asters
you plucked from memory.

I watched you indulge fragilely,
awkwardly in the breath-giving air,
whirling and flouncing
your ponytail and prong hands
as if you needed to feel
that your tattered bones
were still attached to earth.
And the struggle was as much mine,
to settle the restless prattle
that your tongue-slurred wit
and long, shivering pauses stirred in me.

Thinking about you now
and the playhouse moments we shared
years ago, when we picked clovers
for bees we trapped in a Mason jar
and dressed the dolls we made
out of Nehi bottles, wooden clothespins
and braided rope, it seems
you were always like crystal,
kept on a mantel, wanting
and needing to dance in the sun.

Three Creole Women

I. Helen Broussard ("The Popcorn Lady")

Friday nights, her hands were floury and sticky,
buried in mounds as she made her confections,
wrapped them in wax paper, and stacked them
inside a small, foil-lined, cardboard box.

Saturday mornings, she'd knock at my door
wearing her red dress, cradling her pies,
pralines, and popcorn balls. When she smiled,
a garland of marigolds awoke to the sun.

The distant rumble of a freight train faded
in her stories told, like the night she went to a party
and waited to dance, then bent her body
to the weight of the man she later married.

With her gone, I wonder who keeps the recipes,
the measuring cup and rolling pin. Who stirs
the pots and holds a spoon over a bowl of tap water
to drip the hot sugar and cane syrup?

II. Olita Taylor

Words cut like a butcher's knife
those Thursdays when she set two tables.
We rushed past morning to the noon day,
past streets that kept history like broken clocks,
past steel and glass futures rising to a blank sky,
past the squalor of shanty homes that never stop dying,
past the curbside scent of garlic and pork fat,
        her blue-belled hydrangeas playing Duke and Satchmo,
        her splintered pine steps and porch screen flies,
        her wrinkled plaid dress and kiss, dripping sweat,
        the buffet pictures of her babies and wedding day,

the clank and clatter of her pans and black iron pots,
past the talk about movies, sports and breaking news
of murders, disasters and foreign wars,
past the skin, eyes and smiling teeth
of all the angels and demons lurking about,
past the judges, justices and supreme injustices
with their pardons, paroles and death sentences.
Pass me a plate.
Pass some rice and gravy.
Pass the beans, greens and candied yams.
Pass the salt,
Pass the tea
and all the chicken-shit politicians, please.

III. Mary Hebert (On Her 106th Birthday)

You, the old, frail griot, teller of our past,
wearing your skull-knit cap and girly,
lace-collard dress, what can you tell us now,
when your lone candle points like a spire,
flickers like a lighthouse and a cupola
of ringing bells, when your corona beams
bright as the sun, tall as a stela chiseled
from mountain rock or a great oak nesting
a thousand birds? What can you say
for our long, blinded, sand stormy nights,
when your days number the stars, leaping
the centuries of bondage and freedom,
though your country, engendered by war,
struck by color, still searches for its soul?

Mary Louella's Kitchen

My mother seldom cooked without talking
on the telephone. Tucking the receiver
against her sweat-beading cheek and left ear lobe,
she'd stretch the long, black elastic chord

of the wall phone into every corner of the kitchen.
Her arms and hands flapped like a hummingbird
when she chopped and stirred. She splashed gossip
and laughter on the walls for as long as it took

to cook dinner, tidy up her mess, and set the table,
after having stood all day over the greasy broilers
at Mr. Woody's, Mr. Hunter's or other
white-owned restaurants whose food she made

popular. It was the only work she knew.
When she retired, her kidneys failed.
Once, when I had gone to visit during her dying
days of dialysis, she rose from the couch

and began peeling shrimp for okra gumbo
thawing on the counter. Seeing her lean over
the sink, her right foot resting atop the left
to shift the weight of pain, I insisted she not cook.

But she continued, knowing how much I loved
her gumbo. Years later, the house is vacant.
Furniture and boxed keepsakes fill the rooms.
I've taken bric-a-brac, her camera and photos,

and the jean jacket she often wore. But her
kitchen remains intact. Cabinets and drawers full
of dishes, pots, and utensils. Hand notes, mainly
names and phone numbers, still taped to the wall.

Women of Rose Hill

They could be scarecrows
in their torn ragged clothes
reeking of urine and sweat,
or bronze sculptures, posing stiffly
until their arms nimbly jerk and sway.
You might never see them
melting in the quiet stir of morning coffee,
not even their cupped hands
and slurred, fragmented sentences
with commas of saliva dripping
from the corners of their mouths.

If you lean close, you'll hear
their hallelujah-hellos,
as when Bernadette says:
Things got real bad, so I came here.
Dogs walking down the sidewalk
in broad daylight,
going into the stores and banks,
and nobody gave a damn—
snakes and rats crawling everywhere,
even in church. So I came here.
Or out of the blue Lucy blurts:
You're a nice fellow.
That your wife? Where you from?
Hey, got a dollar for a soda pop?
Pay you back. I promise.

Hold on long enough
and you'll climb the steep slope
beyond your centered self
to the sweet jagged ledge
where they dance.

A Cappella

The women of Kairos live far from the sea,
but they know a time in the soul's journey
when stars grow dim and the vessel enters
a bending, swirling strait.
Rising before dawn, together
they step past the armed-man gate,
through doors that lock behind them,
concrete walls enclosed in a tall, iron fence
with thorns curling its top.

They enter the courtyard of Rachel's Garden,
flowers of every kind blooming,
and walk past Jacob's Well.
With shadows lurking in their path,
they climb to an upper room.
Like a net weaved tight and wide,
a ribbon anchoring ship to shore,
they pray their light-bearing psalms,
a cappella into the dark, blinding night.

Vigil

You spent your last days tangled
in the tributaries that drowned
every movement and sound.
No bird song lulled
your wind-borne leaves,
but I knew by the candy red
gloss of your nails that you
had come to die.

The walls of your room paled
like frostbit ground.
A calendar had stopped turning.
Like the tulips Akemie sent
FedEx from Gainsville, the balloon
Orianna brought refused to die.
Sermons and songs stayed muted
in the television hanging above
your bundle of belongings.

I could never tell
what your jaundiced stare saw,
whether my words folded
halves of your heart
or colored the portraits
you might have seen
in kisses to your sweat-beading brow.

In days too long without rain
to keep your gladiolas alive,
the May sun locked
a mandala of hands. Like the grove
blooming outside your window,
we circled your bed.

THREE

... we all came here as candidates
for the slaughter of the innocents.
—James Baldwin

Hunting Dragonflies

If you got lucky you would swat a big one
with a stick that had no other purpose
just after the sun dropped,
when twilight hid the slow pitch.
You would hurry too late
to pinch her thin translucent wings
before she recovered and fluttered,
darting the ghostly plain
even your thoughts would not enter.

One day when a warm beam sealed
the mud pond, you held your breath
and crept through the cattails
to sneak up on a little one,
her wings like brittle leaves.
She wilted in the weight of your hand
until you sighed and let go.
Yet, sooner than you blinked
she crisscrossed the sky,
taking your breath with her,
leaving your scent
dangling like a jingling chime.

If you got lucky, she'd flit right by
your hawk-eyed stare
and tangle in the sweet-briar.
You could reach in—free her
and hold her the way a morning breeze
sways a robin's nest. Instead,
you put her in your darkened room,
the garden of your dreams,
cluttered with the memory
of your daddy's heavy coarse hands
and the thump you felt
swatting into a drowning light.

An Artist Reflects on His Creations

for Xzavion (2004-2012)

I don't name the ones outside
my mirrors, left to drift,
knocking on my doors,
peeking through papery walls

and wooden beams, shuttered
from my memory
to their dying breaths,
the ones I bruise

who break and fall then rise
from the blackened abyss
wearing faces my shadow sheds
to stalk my bedlam dreams,

the ones smitten by light,
who grow to bloom
nobly and picturesque,
sparkling in the city squares,

praying in a thousand tongues
that shatter the cathedral glass.
I name the brown ones,
color them alabaster

to make a pond
reflect a leafy canopy
in a *Sunday Picnic* painting
that can't color pain

of a child in the tree house.
I call him Xzavion,
blood of my blood,
flesh of my flesh,

living inside my mirrors
doors and tearing walls,
my hammering hands
writing a dark song of rage.

Hand-Sewn Dolls

New Year's Day. Sky crisp azure.
Violas sparkling on a blanket
of frost and fallen leaves.
Tinsel still glistening in the pines.

As the sun falls, winter's claws grip
the shanty shot-gun house. Inside,
children lie like loaves.
A faulty space heater crackles,

jetting its flames. No one hears
the cries and screams deafened
by the icy wind whistling
as it rattles the half-caulked panes.

Mornings later, wind still swirls
the ashes. A scent of charred cypress
clings to the mourners
who snake a curbside altar

made of teddy bears, poster boards
and ribbon-tied potted mums.
Nearby, a winterberry tree stands
flush with evergreen and holly.

Driving, I pause to look inside
until the eyes of five hand-sewn
dolls someone had put there
stare back, turning me away.

Cries Beyond the Mountains

for Haiti's Children

I. 1611

Before the sun is born and a cry stirs
the shaman's dream, the gulls give what silence
takes: mating calls fluttering in soft pelting rain,
scatting inside the sweet cradle of eucalypti
that rise above the cloth-draped masts.
But when the sun dies behind granite peaks,
and the oars push slave ships back out to sea,
gulls gather their wings and line the shoal
where footprints of their elders wash away.
Like sand-buried bones, human, broken,
all that remains is what silence gives:
cries drowning in the woodland and churning
in the waves while feathers of ravaged nests
swirl in a pitch-black night.

II. 2011

When hunger is the villagers' anthem and they have
no bread, they curry moons, they break stars.
Their song is in their hands, so they cut wood,
make fire, let heat stretch the drum skins.
Only then do they grip the sticks and beat.
And the world that hears, looks but doesn't see
children coiled on rock-dirt floors,
their coffins lining the wailing streets
while mothers mourn in evensong, fathers migrate
like the plague they carry womb to womb.
Though gulls glide over quicksand shores
and drums beat the villagers into flesh,
there is no peace for these voices, this sky,
this precious rock gleaming wildly in the sea.

Sands of Somalia

For months in Baidoa
the heavens were shut. No crops.
No water from the flinty rock.
Only war and death.
Soldiers sold off our corn rations,
while our babies became skin and bone.
Forty nights we crossed the desert.
Our feet blistered,
so we made the daylight sand our bed.

One morning while we slept,
rebels ambushed. They beat me
and took the last of our food.
We thought of going back
but we had to press on.
Then, late one night a week ago,
I watched my daughter die.
We buried her in the sand
with our hands, with only our prayers
to mark her grave.
The moon, big as the sun,
made the white sands sparkle
so brightly I felt
we walked inside the stars,
but with Nadifa gone,
everything shining
drowned in our tears.

Here at the camp we must wait.
Too many need help.
My wife is going mad now,
and our youngest is very sick.
He breathes from his belly—
no sound, not even a cry, only air.
Look. His skull sinks in.
See. Put your hand here.
Feel the hole.

Samuel and Solomon, Age Six

Such a hard thing to understand,
the newspaper headline quoted
the boys' uncle as saying.
Perhaps the photographs pulled me
inside—a snapshot of the boys,
their arms raised high,
tiny specks of light beaming
in the center of their black marble eyes,
brightening their broad smiles
with cheeks bulging like buds
waiting to bloom.

And the photo of the processional:
young black men, two to a side,
flanking two small boxes.
With heads bowed, they grip
the shiny chrome handles
of the baby blue caskets
draped with white carnations.
Like Samuel and Solomon,
the men wear white gloves,
pink shirts and blue neckties,
no jackets, no pinned boutonnieres.

A short drive from the maple-lined field
dotted with gray tombstones,
red, yellow and white roses,
the mother sits in county jail.
The news reports how, not why,
she killed them, then tried to kill herself.

Now, four years later,
as I've pulled this faded, torn newspaper
from a dresser drawer

half-filled with laminated memories,
these images, like bulbs once buried
and forgotten inside the cold,
lifeless ground of winter,
sprout in the warm blush of June.

Quicksand

After school, only us children
were home. We sat
inside a deep, roadside ditch
talking to the chinch bugs,
listening to the boom and clang
of box cars switching rails.
We threw china balls at hoboes
who leapfrogged the thicket.

Once, I drifted inside
your mama's screened back porch
and saw a pair of trousers
strewn across a chair. I turned
the knob of the nearest shut door
and found a man covering
you like a morphing cloud.

I didn't know I had seen
your soul tumbling, and I would
become the faceless doll
of all your wet-bed dreams.

She never grew up, that child
inside you, whose broken years
took their toll pretending
to be whole, clutching
the ragged sleeve and quicksand
lining of her daddy's wool top coat.

The Girl Inside

I. The Rooftop, Ninth Ward, New Orleans

I just keep thinking what Granny told me:
Close your eyes, Autumn.
Whatever you do, don't look
down. Just pretend
you're not here.
So I shut my eyes and squeeze my hands
like sponge balls, tight as I can.
I'm so scared
I can't feel my body.
All I can see is black,
like being underground.
I've never been underground,
but I've been in rooms
with no lights on
and I had to pop my eyes wide open
just to see something.

I feel my body coming back
now, as my feet leave the roof.
I'm in the sky,
going *up, up, up,*
yet it feels more like a tunnel.
The hard wind stings my face.
My ears hurt, too.
I can't stop trembling.
My body shakes all over—my jaws,
my arms, my legs.
I pretend I am a bird
flapping my wings
up, up, up
toward the sun.

II. The Superdome

The helicopter brought us here.
We sleep on the floor.
I keep waiting for the police
to come back and take us home.
I lie on my backpack
with my hands behind my head
and look up at the high ceiling,
counting the bright lights in the circle—
101, 102, 103, 104, 105.
The more I look up
the brighter the lights get,
the smaller my body feels.

The boy next to me keeps throwing up
and his nose bleeds. He's curled up
and resting his head in his sister's arms.
He could die here, his sister says.
She says they slept on a bridge last night.
They saw dead people floating in the water.
One time, I saw a bug in Granny's back yard.
I watched his tiny legs crawl to the leaves,
then I poked him with a stick
and he also curled into a ball.

Now, it stays dark in here all the time.
I don't know why.
Stay close to me, Autumn, Granny says.
Don't move, stay put.
I'm hungry.
They don't feed us or give us any water.
I feel like a big rock is pulling me down,
way down, under the ground.
The air stinks in here, too,
so I hold my breath as long as I can.

All these shouts and screams
and popping sounds scare me.
But I try not to get scared.
Am I going to die?

Then, I look up and remember
I'm a little girl.
I've been here before
in a wave.
I remember seeing it come
from the other side,
watching it roll, waiting
to throw my body inside it
at just the right second.
I slid to the edge of my chair
and held my arms out, then
up, up, up.
I didn't want to let it go.
When it passed, I was still rolling.

III. Bus Ride

The soldiers came to get us.
But I don't know where we're going.
Out the window, I see
nothing but houses and trees
knocked down.
Everything is in the river,
even cars and trucks!
When I look down, I wonder:
Is this where the boy and his sister slept?
Is this where they saw dead people
floating in the water?

IV. Renaissance Village

I live in a trailer now.
It's crowded where I sleep,
and it feels stuffy all the time,
like I'm in a playhouse.
I can hardly breathe
inside. I don't want to talk
or even look at people.
People I know, like my best
friend Tamika, are gone,
but I know
one day I'll be gone, too.
I'll curl myself into a ball
and roll far out into the sea,
or I'll fly away,
up, up, up,
looking straight at the sun.

Tree Poem

for Jeremiah

I.

Your father died a month short of your third year,
four months after Hurricane Katrina.
Driving to Hattiesburg for his funeral, I watched
the flat land roll softly into the hills.
All the pines lay stiffly on the ground.

That morning, in the vestibule behind the sanctuary,
I sat with you and your brothers, waiting.
Jeremiah, stop running, I repeated.
Stop pushing, Jeremiah.
Joseph, leave him alone.
When they closed the casket, we went inside
to sit with the family.
No one wanted to cry aloud,
the air eerie as the eye of a storm.

II.

One hot summer day when you were five,
we drove to the mall. I know Autumn felt left out,
but I wanted to go shopping with only the boys.
The boulevard of the main entrance was old,
but the tall palm trees had just been planted.
Even I felt in a different place, wondering
why the branches still stood tied.

You sat in the back seat between Joseph and James,
while John Elisha sat up front.
Who has been here before? I asked,
to which you answered, *Not me, Paw Paw.*
When we shopped, you didn't want the same color
as Joseph's, so you picked green plaid short pants

with lines that clashed with the abstract design
of your pale green shirt. It said nothing
and everything about you.

III.

Jeremiah, you *had* been to the mall before,
with your brothers and me,
three days before your father's funeral.
The palm trees hadn't been planted yet.
But it was Christmastime.
Wreaths and red ribbons decked the boulevard,
and you saw Santa and bright-colored lights.
Like a butterfly fluttering on a blossoming bough,
you perched atop the carousel horse,
then flitted through the aisles of the toy store.

I know you don't remember. In time you may
hurt, even without the memory of your father.
Will you know his goodness and understand
why he took his life? Will you forgive him?
Will you stand tall in all seasons,
your branches blooming strong and wide?

When we left the mall, we went to the Mississippi River
and stood on the levee to watch barges
drag the current. Like logs, we rolled our bodies
down the steep slope, our arms raised high,
giving ourselves to the ground and open air.

Picture Day at Mount Pilgrim, 1957

Blackbirds perch on every stalk
of the bean garden,
their eyes open wide
for this still morning shot.

Little one in the front row,
I see your wooden stare,
       hanky balled tightly,
       your sister's Sunday-worn socks,
       feet barely touching down
       with loose-buckled shoes,
       worn and cracked
       like your grandma's hands,
       a story in every line,
       like this morning
       when she warmed the iron,
       one by one gathered
       and pressed the cancan pleats
       that drape your pebbled knees.
I see the ribbon she unraveled
to bow-tie the braids she curled
thinking. . .

Any minute, child, the taxi will blow.
Ms. Gillespi's sheets need wash
and I ain't even soaked my feet yet.

Colored girl,
       someday you'll know why
       miles away in Little Rock,
       at this hour,
       time stopped
       and warriors marched
       only to a drummer's beat
       with a steady bird's-eye aim
       on freedom.

Look up!

FOUR

What did I know, what did I know
Of love's austere and lonely offices?
—Robert Hayden

Torched

Grandmother wind whirled,
screaming prayer to the stars.
Granddad circled half-moon
to a crucifix in her eyes,
uttered something damning,
then raised his palm
and slapped water out of her.

He had been at the sea wall all day,
shoving ice for boats that stirred
the Atchafalaya's deep roux silt.
His feet sloshed inside wet wool socks,
rubber boots up to his knees.
His beans and salt meat still warmed
on the hot water heater.

Like a patient soprano,
fire shattered the glassy night,
leaping from the rooftop
to teary willows swaying
to an old fashioned freedom song.
Memories flashed of time he had spent
in the iron-bending Angola sun,
the deaf drum of a wooden bench
against his skull, how it felt
to butcher a man
as easy as cards turned flush,
feeling his hands blister and swell
in a sweat dripping dream
and not levitate and free-fall
with her scent clinging to him.

What's one torched sky
to a life branded by color
and days that can't be counted,
loving the only way
a once caged heart can?

Hand Fan

My natural father and I had no relationship.
When my mother got pregnant
at 15, he married her, then
enlisted in the Army,
hoping the farm girl and her baby
would somehow disappear.
By the time he returned, we had.
The most he ever said to me:
a letter praising my manhood,
expressing his regrets,
sent fifteen years before he died.

When he died, his body arrived
at the church an hour late.
The funeral director, a Rick James
look-alike, wet fake braids,
sequined skin-tight suit and all,
said the hearse had needed washing.

My aunt Nola, 85, a devout Catholic,
still driving, smoking and playing the slots,
sat behind me at the funeral service,
up front in the amen, help-me-Jesus pews,
where mourners hollered and swooned
when the choir sang *Amazing Grace.*

Her hand fan, vintage cardboards
worn thin, edges bent and torn,
loosely tacked to a thin wooden stick,
flapped left to right, right to left,
pulling and pushing a soft breeze.
On one side, the mortuary's seal,

on the other, a hand-sketched portrait
of Rev. Martin Luther King, Jr.
"Damn shame," she stiffly muttered,
leaning over my shoulder.
"That preacher know damn well
your daddy wasn't that good."

Gazing

One King Holiday, I wheeled you
to the nursing home patio.
Drifting in and out of your blank stare,
I read Trethewey's "Southern History,"
recalling the year at Rosteet Junior High
when Ms. Troutman, the Civics teacher,
said Hoover was right to call King
a Communist. That was a lie,
I knew, but enough to make
Hugh Morton and his pals hate more.

That year, the one before King's death,
a bad spine kept you home
for weeks. On those mornings,
I rose early to cook two eggs for you
over easy. Keeping the flame low
and blue beneath the old black skillet,
I dragged the spatula slowly
to gather the frothing butter,
careful not to break the yolk
nor harden the thin white.
Across town, Mama's polished
corn-slit shoes and air-dried nylon dress
had already stained with grease
from Mr. Woody's hot oven broiler.

Daddy, gazing into your eyes,
the longleaf swaying
as the sun's yolk peeked
through gray clouds behind you,
I wondered if I'd ever really known
the burden you bore:
a black man living in the South.

The Shaving Mirror

I arrive late with the intent of leaving early.
You have eaten dinner, and your body knows
the hour has passed for you to be strapped to a pulley,
hoisted from your chair and laid to bed until morning.
But I find pleasure in holding your face
in my hand, a son's indulgence—
to put sweetened bread within your reach
like a teething toy, then lean over
your drooping torso and groom you,
tugging at your stiffened neck,
your fingers grabbing and pinching like claws.

Your face in my hand—
once child's play, now darkened, tarnished glass.
Shaving your gray, stubborn stubbles, I hum
a tuneless song to the bee-like drone
of a Norelco. I polish the roughness
that pricks my palm, finding
a dimly glaring image, a moment not many
years ago, when a gentle, loving man calmly rose
from his chair, stood stiffly on his legs
and spoke my name, and I knew
his stone-like look meant *I am the father.*

Theinessen Pond

Where my father once lived, I stroll
the banks of a man-made pond
full of fish that don't jump.
At night, the old man wandered outdoors.
I feared he would slip into the water,
so I moved him to another home,
where he fell and broke his hip,
never to walk again.

Seen from the south in the midday sun,
the pond hangs framed like a landscape portrait,
as if it were nighttime and the fish have died
and the sky doesn't sing so crystal blue
that it shatters in my eyes.

When I drift to the other side, beyond
the ducks circling a mound of cattails,
the surface sparkles and glitters,
but I see neither land nor water, only
two worlds colliding. Time
is not when but where, and truth
as much what I can't see as what I believe.

Tears

You always seemed to wear a mask.
The day we buried Mama,
you stood like a guard, gazing
steadfast and straight ahead,
as though you were not lost
and needed no help
to find your way.
But in your dry-eyed calm,
your words stuttered,
your shirt and tie didn't match,
and one small tear ran
down the seam
of your wrinkled pants.

Growing up, I never saw you cry.
If I had, you wouldn't have allowed me
to reach in and touch
the drops streaming,
rub their silky softness
between my fingers, then brush them
across your stiff, bristled face.

Today, you are the child—all body
and sounds without words.
Before the Christmas party,
the nursing assistant dressed you
in someone else's pants and boots.
She put you in the flannel plaid shirt
you had often worn
when you tinkered with your engines.
As you sat in the wheelchair and ate,
your body slouching to one side,
you sank more deeply

into a valley without laughter.
Like melted snow, tears at last
flowed, bursting the banks
of a long, winding, ancient river.

My Father's Treasures

Years ago, his day always ended
with a question mark-shaped hook
behind a narrow, shut door,
where he slipped out of the grime
and grit of the train tracks,
settling to a table Mama had set.

His big denim overalls were heavy,
oily, smelled of sweat and daylong sun,
pockets too deep
for a child's hands. I dug
slowly into them,
sifted sandy pebbles,
the crumpled paper
and loose fibers.
Fumbling his pocket knife,
a clump of ringed keys,
I gently quieted the tinkling taps,
then took few enough coins
not to be missed,
thinking no grown man
would count change so small.

Now, when I watch
his thin, weathered hands
cling to a table top corner,
I feel his mind groping,
grazing bare, slumbering fields,
taking what little he finds.

Crossing

I.

Workdays you tiptoed the high wire
and steep cliff ledge, wearing blue twill
and a bright orange vest,
each crosswalk a sea, a compass, a cargo of children.
Still, Earth passed you by
with time pieces you strapped
to each wrist for trips to Texas and California,
circling city blocks and returning home.

"Something has fallen out of my head,"
you said, just weeks before
Katrina made bones of the city
and broke the hand of Jesus.
When Rita came exhaling,
I begged you to leave,
but you stayed—half-beast, half-child,
living in no-man's-land.

You resisted my tearing down
the great wall you built of ants,
souring pots and junk mail.
One morning I pulled a drawer
and found your pistol, old vials of blue pills
and years of unspent cash.

II.

Stars drown
in the black drone of waves.

                          You cross
                          in cold light.
                          You lie down
                          with newborn fields

and scented voices,
a titter and a word
short of laughter.
Hands lock in a mudra.
We feed you.

Old vessel, sweet daemon,
do we cage you crib-like
to protect you from yourself?
Or is it the delicate crystal within
we fear?

A Stranger Loss

for Stephen W. Cavanaugh

I seldom think about the river
that sleeps beside the city,
but I shun crossing its tallest bridge.
Today, I climbed it
in a chrome-polished black limousine,
thinking about my uneven cuffs
and clumsily pinned boutonniere,
wondering why someone stood
strangely at the top on the ledge.
I recalled a day that broke
months ago, when I sat
looking down on a different city—
lush hills, steep streets, a scent of fish
and sea to dream by.
Suddenly, an email: *Steve Cavanaugh*
has pancreatic cancer.
Doctors give him three to six months.

Steve, in that choked-breath moment,
a distant foghorn
lifted wayward stars
we often searched sitting
like logs splintering in a dying fire
our generation had been given to kindle.
In twenty years of friendship,
I never knew your political party
and didn't hear your recitations
of Chaucer and Seuss.
Through all our God-talk
and bush-burning muse,
I never knew where you worshipped.
Until today, when they covered you
in a bed of irises west of the river,
I had not cried the loss of anyone
of a race other than my own.

FIVE

You're a genie in disguise.
Full of wonder and surprise.
— From *Betcha By Golly, Wow*
Tom Bell and Linda Creed
Sung by The Stylistics

Rain Dance

In all your years, you never knew
that long before your words
named me,
I tossed my tiara
and shimmering bodice
to dance the songs
you had yet to sing.

When you first saw me,
I was a young girl
streaking half-naked
across your back yard
just before the bus horn blew,
quick as lightning flashed.
Now, in your dying,
you still wonder
if you were dreaming then.
*Was she
there? Was she
rain bathing or fleeing
some man's hands?*

You called me mama, wife,
your secret lover
who gathered hay, milked the herd
and made a bed where you laid
your hollow self down.
I strung beads,
weaved my round skirt
and spun you
the way drunkenness forgets.

Zydeco on Dog Hill

Before they put Cousin Gladys
inside the ground in a cornrow
of fair-skinned Creole men, I sat
in her funeral mass imagining
two shadows dancing in the swish
of a swift moving blade
that slit her dreams in half
and sent her father strolling
across the cane field
like a land-bending river, turning
a page she could never turn back:
news that a man had been killed,
her husband had been jailed.
I heard spoons scratching
a washboard, and a zydeco
accordion pump a groove
through a sweat-dripping rumble
of fast-shuffling feet. I felt
the wooden floor turn to water
and tasted the salty wave
as Jo Jo, her lover, swung out,
flaunting his gabardine
in two tones, his wide brim
fedora suddenly seen
whirling in a herd of flamingos
and a pool of whiskey-warm blood.

Memphis Soul Hour

Nights my grandpa gambled,
grandma lay awake
with her rosary beads
draped to the bed post.
Dragging heavy, crusted
feet, she'd rise to open
her door, squeaking,
and let all the bone heat
of hell fly. Chewing clumps
of corn starch, she'd rattle
her teeth like a tin can.
On the living room couch
two daughters slump
with their lovers
while Memphis Soul crackles
softly in the blue-lit dark.
Sultry and sweaty, they slither
like snakes between
whispers and a sex wish.
Then, a tongue spewing
holy water and fire,
a soliloquy of cuss and prayer
seething like boiling grits.
Sheetrock walls shimmy,
porch screen hinges pop,
and a breeze cools the house.

My Brother's Flowers

for Victor Hebert

I wasn't there the night
he shattered the glass door
and set Mr. Bob's bike shop on fire,
but I knew he was burning hate
and not the steel wool and oil
that turned our rims into rhinestones.
And I wasn't there the night
he sped through the whorish fields
into all the years he hadn't lived,
playing chase with a trooper
as he swallowed white pills
and a half ounce of redbud,
or when his lover's husband
snapped a .38 at his head
and the barrel swallowed air.
I didn't stand with him
on the steep, jagged cliffs,
in closets he entered
before looking inside.
But I listened to him
reasoning in his obsessions,
moaning midnight blues
by quiet fires he lit
of letters from Debbie, ashes
settling like dust in his soul,
lilies blooming where he cried.

Karaoke

She could have been his
baby girl if, thirty years ago,
he had met her mama
serving sake at a Karaoke bar.
Her satin lips, glossy
against her pale, long cheeks,
rock him like a wind chime,
strumming a concerto
that only he can hear
in the backwoods of Alabama.
He sits bobbing on a carousel
while liquor talks to his head
like the prattle of her costume
jewelry and Little Dippers
painted on her nails.
Staring down a highball,
he recalls a day long ago
when he found thumb-size photos
of nude Asian women
in his daddy's bottom drawer,
and ghosts he saw
when he held the old Kodak
negatives to a light. Looking up
now, he sees only stars
clinging to a bulging blouse,
and words he can't read.

Baptism

One Sunday night we swayed
in a holy wind, wearing *Super Fly*
shirts and Eleganza shoes
we had seen at the Palace Theatre.
Life reeled in front of milk crate squats,
between reefers and the poison
we gulped out of cheap port wine
mixed with fruit juice and spit.
Hitched a ride with a Viet Nam vet
turned hustler, whose Brougham,
half-primed, half-painted, choked
like a bleeding hog, blasting funk
from a plywood, shag-covered box:
Curtis, Santana, and our favorites—
soft horns and violins, high tenors
telling of broken hearted men
and love we dreamt of making.
Peach-fuzzed and celluloid,
we cruised over Cyclops' bridge,
crept alleyways that stunk of piss,
and stood at a slut's bedside.
Would-be-gangbangers, candles
flickering on a frosted cake, we circled
her nakedness like a prayer vigil—
Awestruck. Eyes bulging. Legs
buckling on a thin sheet of lake ice.

Foghorn

Ambrosia, fine wine, petals
on his pillow. On his mind,
the sound her body gives,
while fog spills and seeps
through an open window,
covering like a white silk sheet.
He's inside a dream:
a bar in London. Smoke
blankets the keys that mock
whining blue notes
of her cat-meow muted horn,
a rendition of Ella Fitzgerald's *All of You*.
A pitter-patter percussion drags
oily droplets of bass thumping
softly inside a damp mossy hush,
while a voice scats feathery
in the distance. He feels a bite,
a burn at the cliff edge of pain.
There'll be blue lights,
doors she can't unlock,
a song she'll play forever,
but she wants to go all the way,
cross the line, hear him moan
like he did their first time,
when the record scratched
and he screamed for mercy.

White Night at the Willow Lounge

Sitting at the bar, aloof,
country crooning in my ear,
absorbed inside my reflections
and shadowboxing self-hate,
I caught a glimpse of a woman
on the dance floor, spraying mace
into a man's eyes. My eyes lit
the exit sign, then I heard gun shots
and a wave rolling, crashing
like a high-speed train. Something
gave me wings and lifted me
out the door, where the tip
of a handgun barrel, bobbing
like a house fly,
landed on my forehead.
Through Death's waxwork-eyes
and hazy glass wall,
I was phantom and fog,
a fawn astray at a forest glade.
His finger coiled on the trigger,
I knew he needed to shoot again
to kill the smallness
she had made him feel,
the strong man
he had not measured up to.
He needed to feed a hunger within
and find his way out
of the black hole that pulled him
down the belly of a whale.
In his mind the icy weight of steel,
belief ablaze, the betrayal
of a soft assuring touch, and me,
watching him fade into the cold,
white night, giving back my life,
like the Trickster in a dream.

SIX

To everything there is a season,
and a time to every purpose under heaven.
—Ecclesiastes 3:1

Lessons Learned from a Teenage Daughter

for Karen

Once, while riding with you into the horizon,
I saw a dab of light on the tip of a fine brush,
long and handless. In the blink of an eye,
the brush, with a single stroke, painted
a yellow sickle perfect in its arc
across a plain of purplish hues.

I had always known a time would come
when you would not need my permission
to follow the voice that answers
whether you should go here or there.
I had hoped that in whatever hour or season
a dim light spoke you would discern
right from wrong. Like the tale told
of children who stood before the old, wise
blind woman with a bird in their hands,
the voice you found was your own.

On a day that would have been perfect
but for your discontent with my sternness,
I recollected those fire-breath moments
when your grandmother and I argued
petty rightness as you and I often did.

In wiser years, how nice that we grow
together to watch chameleon, mosaic skies
and let pains die that we might have cried
and hidden in raindrops sprinkling
on a starless night without a kiss surrendered.
God knows those nights are long.

Dream Walk

Andre´ spoke plainly through bottled memories
of nights a jail hammer numbed his head,
mornings his hands bled on the plow
and he prayed the okra survived the storm.

He spoke broken French and counted
only pocket change and cards those evenings
when he cocked his chapeau in a quarter moon
and stepped out with a pipe full of Bugle.

To him Rose was soufflé, fresh meringue, a breeze
on his backside when he kicked his heels
to a caramel sky and swayed with her
the way jelly rolled when she walked.

Early one Sunday, while silver shimmered
on the coulee's bank, he stepped out
of bed into a dream that lured him to the woods,
near the honky-tonk joint where men stood

outdoors huddled around smoking pits.
He watched them signify about their blues,
bemoaning their lost loves. Then, in the caged
cry of a crow's caw, a hound's howl,

and buck shots splattering leaves, he shot
and killed two cottontails, tied them to a bough,
emptied their bellies and stripped their coats.
Later that night, long after Rose heard

the last crackle of the oven cooling,
he kicked his boots at her door,
dripping murky water—rabbits in one hand,
and a long string of catfish in the other.

Blue Moments

My second trip home from the garden center.
The aroma of crawfish etouffe at the door.
Narva at the kitchen table, leaning over
an empty plate and a tall ice tea.

I didn't tell her how good it felt
when the cute little clerk at the checkout
had wiped the sweat off my face
with a cool wet towel
and said she always helps her man
when he works in the yard,
and the clerk standing beside her winked
and said, *I rub my man's neck and shoulders
after a hard day's work, has his food cooked
and the table set. It's fifty-fifty.*

Resisting self-pity, I told them
that Narva had been in church all morning
praying for the world and me,
and she'd spent the day before
spring cleaning. An hour later,
when she pulled out of the garage
and rolled down the window
to say she and a girlfriend were going
to a festival, I was ankle-deep
in cypress mulch and cow manure.
Perfume filled the air as she sped away.

And the festival t-shirt she promised me?
Only one left in your size, she said
upon returning, *but I didn't buy it.
I've never seen you in that shade of blue.*

Between After and Before
(The House of Ernest and Mathilda)

Watching her come awake, he wondered
if they grew too familiar with bluebird songs
and soft bursting light. What is that sound
they'd hear on winter mornings, when darkness lingered
and the blinds were shut tight? They didn't know
the gardenias had bloomed early outside
their bedroom window and petals had fallen
patiently to the frosty leafy ground. Where
is the scent and silence that paced the splintering fire
that settled the rafters and caused the walls to knock
high above them, while their bodies floated
on a stream of hot spring water? They didn't care
where the knock went or when it would come again.
They lay still, feeling the dawn move.

*

Every house has a space called the corner of time
for things old and forgotten, time to step back
to how the world used to be, until a blind folds,
a light flickers and fades. He does that with his life,
gathers what he has made of it, subtracts what is lost,
recalls moments he could have lived differently,
when her heart tugged for what he didn't give.

Just before dawn, she sits whispering devotions
beside a dim glowing lamp. He sits outdoors,
inside the other darkness, listening blindly
to mating calls tweeting on the tree top,
knowing he'll see the sparrows when dawn rises
and they'll glide and streak by him in pairs.
To him, time is a door, a window he never shuts.

*

One Sunday afternoon, they left home walking.
They strolled past the geese pond, entered a chapel
hidden in the oak grove and sat on a wooden bench.
They wandered curiously into a mansion half-built
with a steep stair and dusty floors, rooms they lost
count of. That evening, after the rain subsided,
they talked and touched. Then came silence,
what she didn't say, drowning his hopes and prayers
like the unsearchable knock in the walls.

A cold still form, his body, the boy figurine
with a heart adrift like blood in a bottle
cast to sand and waves, where the only sound
is his, and her silence, trenchant as rain
shattering rock, thunder dimming a wayward star.

*

Alone in the woods, he thinks about her and time,
something he once said or didn't say that turned
to ice or stone or brittle winter leaves rustling
across a pebbled walkway, crackling like fire
in the gentle push of a ground breeze,
crushed under steps of strangers passing.

Above him, tall half-brown maples whisk and hum
in a pendulum. In the distance, the rat-a-tat
bounce of a ball, an annoying stream of engines.

With her that afternoon, the room had no floor or ceiling.
He listened to the heart's drum, a pounding hush
of doubt and disbelief. As day moved, she went
to the window and touched the dry potted soil, then
she watered the ivy wilting, bending gently toward light.

*

Today the cardinals feed and flutter in the puddle ponds.
He'll fill a basket and spread flowers in Mallard Park
on a thick bed of sloping grass, thistle, and wild trees.
Just days before, when rain spoiled their picnic,

he opened the blinds and laid a quilt on a hardwood
floor in front of their glass French doors. Twenty patches
in bloom, none the same. He thought they made
a perfect square until he walked the striped borders
and counted five rows of four. Ten pink and white
poke-a-dot roses, each with two leaves. Five red tulips
and five paisley roses, each with one leaf. Watching her,
he thought, *she was this way when he first saw her eyes*
gleaming, imagining, believing. The quilt maker
must have knelt and stitched prayers in the seams.

*

Sunday morning, almost noon, sky slate gray.
She surprised him with an offer to ride
a hundred miles to see his uncle. He drove listening
to a recorded sermon. She solved word puzzles,
read the story of Rahab the prostitute, then slept.
His uncle looked scrubby but had started eating again,
back to saying *yeah,* the one word he remembered.

Returning home, they stopped at Fresh Produce Market,
and for less than five dollars bought enough fruit
and fresh roasted peanuts to fill her bowl and his.
At Jerry's Bistro they sipped wine over burgers and fries.
He listened to her excitement about baking cookies
for women prisoners. *You didn't see it,* she said,
but the sun peeped before it set. You were driving east.

*

Alone, he spent one night at the vacant home of his boyhood,
made a makeshift bed and heard no sound
except blue flames jutting the burner of an old
iron space heater. Driving from central Louisiana,
he had taken Hwy 165 South, which at one point parted
the Kisatchie National Forest. Past the protected wild,
the road grew. Buildings sat where tall
slender pines once stood straight as water towers
named of small towns the rails and crop mills made.
Folks in those parts say a tree is like a hog; nothing
goes to waste. Even so, the trees had been cut down
and the timber plant stretching a mile behind the spur
was closing. The de-barkers, slice saws, and lathes
would be turned off. Workers would be sent home.

*

Ever since he saw the golden fan petals of a ginkgo,
he had been struck by flowers blooming high above ground.
He had hoped for a day in February when they'd see
the lavender of Japanese Magnolia before it fell.

That day, they attended a funeral and strolled the cemetery,
a sling's shot from the fence that he and the Project boys
once climbed to steal pears before he slit his knee
on a broken bottle. The morning drive had taken them across
the steep Sunshine Bridge through cypress swampland
and towns girded by dirt levees holding the Atchafalaya
River.

It was Friday, the eve of Valentine's Day. Pink roses,
white gold, lobster at Chelsie's. Before dinner he prayed
questions. He was at the front door and didn't hear her at
first, until she sat him down folding answers into his hands.

*

Silence left in February, the dying days
of winter. Now, like water seeping merciless rock,

they listen and touch, and every moment
inside them passes between after and before,

the time when lavender blooms, cardinals feed,
and seedlings sow where earth is bare and frostbit.

Years will pass. They will see ponds and trees
and unfinished houses around the corner, an old

wooden chapel in the woods. They will pray,
gather leaves and grow flowers, drive into

a gray horizon with sunset peeping behind.
Like memory and dawn, death will heal,

wheat will bloom, and birdsongs will light
the rooms of their house. Time will love.

About the Author

John Warner Smith's poems have appeared in *Ploughshares*, *Callaloo*, *Antioch Review*, *The Worcester Review*, *River Styx*, *Bloodroot*, *Pembroke*, *Fourteen Hills*, *American Athenaeum*, *Quiddity* and other literary journals. Smith's debut poetry collection was a finalist in the 2013 Crab Orchard Series in Poetry First Book Award competition. His short collection, "Hunting Dragonflies," was a finalist in the 2012 Poetry Contest of the Tennessee Williams / New Orleans Literary Festival. Smith earned his MFA in Creative Writing at the University of New Orleans. He and his wife Narva live in Baton Rouge.